Quintessentially
Nigerian
Food

Simply At Its Best

Dr. Olajumoke Adeloye

AuthorHouse™
1663 Liberty Drive
Bloomington, IN 47403
www.authorhouse.com
Phone: 1-800-839-8640

Published by AuthorHouse 02/07/2012

ISBN: 978-1-4678-8009-1 (sc)

authorHOUSE®

Dedication

Thank you YAHWEH for the ability, gift and grace to complete this work. I give it all back to YOU. We as a family, love food, notably good food! I would therefore, like to give a massive shout out to my parents Dr and Mrs Adeloye, sisters Nike and Tope and brother Yemi. Thanks for all your loving support and kindness, without which this project would not have been possible. There are no recipes like mum's recipes!

Table of Contents

Foreword

It is a difficult thing to write the Foreword for the work of one's child, not least because one is naturally torn between being objective and critical, on one hand, and being adulatory and panegyric that the child has achieved such a feat, on the other. It is against this background that I am really delighted that Olajumoke has given me the honour of writing the Foreword for her new book and I will try my best to strike a decent balance between the two extremes. The new book on Nigerian food is to my knowledge one of a few of its kind and is really useful because of the increasing number of new generation Nigerians in the Diaspora, some of whom have never been to Nigeria, not to talk of being acquainted with Nigerian traditional dishes. I say this because I have personal experience in our family (in which Olajumoke grew up) where it is always a tug of war to get some of the children (definitely not Olajumoke..., but the culprits know themselves!) to take Nigerian foods. Using a simple, easy-to-follow writing approach and abundant colour photographic illustrations, Olajumoke has succeeded in my view to make Nigerian foods appealing to all. The easily set out recipes, cooking and serving instructions are highly useful for Diaspora Nigerians and non-Nigerians alike. How I wish samples could be available to test when the book finally goes on sale!

Dr Olajumoke Adeloye (to use her correct title) is a qualified Medical Doctor and one wonders how she has been able to juggle the demands of her professional job with preparing the manuscript for this excellent book! However, all I do know is that she is a true Nigerian and although she moved to the UK while she was still very young, she has continued to like everything Nigerian, especially of her Yoruba tribe, including the dress, food and culture. It is therefore no wonder that the recipes in the book unashamedly have a Yoruba bias. Nonetheless, I think the book serves all tastes, Yoruba and non-Yoruba, and is also an invitation to non-Nigerians to try out Nigerian foods and make them a regular component of their menu.

To conclude, "Quintessentially Nigerian Food - Simply at its Best" is a must-have book for all Nigerians and non-Nigerians alike and I commend it to all those with the love of good, nourishing foods that Olajumoke has so much enjoyed for a long, long, long time!

Adebayo J. Adeloye

Edinburgh, 2011

Preface and Acknowledgements

At last! Finally, a recipe book that I believe truly represents the majority of the food we so enjoy as Nigerians. This book has been a couple of years in the making but an absolute pleasure to compose. Some of the greatest things arise from the most mundane. It was a Monday morning and my brother and I were making a treacherous journey in the car back home, sliding most of the way back on black ice! It was the winter before he was to start university and it just dawned on me that – what would he cook? And what would he eat? You know? When mum's not there with every plate ready at every meal time, as once had been the case. I was in the midst of recommending a chef's recipe book to him when, it dawned on me! It would be great if he could have a copy of Nigerian recipes to take away to university with him! Hence, this book.

I bet there are many in this exact same situation. I know that when I left home for university some ten years ago, I wasn't sure that I'd manage to make all those loved home recipes. Also, even now I often make these dishes when I'm entertaining friends or if I'm asked to bring a plate to a get-together. I love to cook and it brings me such joy to express this through these dishes that both excite and please the palate. It actually rather astounds me the number of people that I've met who have tasted, attempted to make and love Nigerian food. I cannot count the number of times I've heard 'I wish I knew how to make – Jollof rice, -Fried rice, -Stew! And the list goes on.

In making this book I have attempted to simplify some of our most renowned dishes. I am very liberal in the way I eat them, for example putting some stew on chips as I please. So relax and enjoy working your way through each and every dish.

A big, big, big thanks to my mother and close friend, who so kindly shared her cooking tips and secrets. The best thing about this book of recipes is that it is as traditional as is possible but has my own personal take on things. Thanks to my father who wrote the preface. Additionally my family as a whole also helped proofread this work. I did all my own photography, which I hope you'll appreciate as you go through the book.

As the Yoruba people would say 'Ẹ gbá'dùn oúnj yín o!', which translated in English means 'Enjoy your food'.

The Essential Things

So what are the necessary things you will need? There are some things that are an absolute must for cooking these dishes and some that you can improvise on. I have actually created an equipment list to accompany each recipe but just in case you need to dash out and purchase some of the things you don't have, here is a more comprehensive one.

Kitchen Equipment:

Assortment of sizes of mixing bowls
Baking tray
Blender with mill and pulse functions
Chopping board
Colander
Egg slicer
Igbako (wooden serving spatula)
Kitchen foil
Knives
Ladle
Large measuring jug
Measuring cups
Measuring spoons
Medium and large frying pan
Metal Grater
Metal tongs
Metal whisk
Old newspaper
Orogun (wooden pounding spoon)
Pastry brush
Pastry cutters
Potato masher
Pressure cooker
Rolling pin
Sieve
Slotted spoon
Small, medium and large saucepans
Stirring spoon
Tin foil
Weighing jug

Stew and Soups

These dishes are classic and are to be consumed with dishes in the rice and staples section of this book.

Obe Ata

Serves 4-6

Ingredients:

- 8 pieces Meat/Chicken or 1Kg weight
- 1 Small onion
- 1 Chicken and 3 Maggi stock cubes
- 1 ½ tsp Mild curry powder
- 1 tsp All purpose seasoning
- 1 ½ tsp Thyme
- ½ tsp Garlic powder
- ½ tsp Chilli powder
- 200mls Water to boil the meat/chicken

For blending:
- 400g Tin of plum tomato
- 1 Medium onion
- 1 Medium red pepper
- ½ - 2 Scotch bonnet
- 10mls Tomato puree
- 100ml Water

- 1 Chicken and 2 Maggi stock cubes
- ½ tsp Chilli powder
- 150mls Vegetable/Sunflower oil

Equipment:

- Food blender
- Medium saucepan
- Stirring spoon
- Baking tray
- Tin foil
- Measuring jug
- Slotted spoon

Cooking guide:

Step 1:
- Boil:
    o Rinse the pieces of meat/chicken in cold water and place in the medium saucepan
    o Add the 1 chicken and 3 Maggi stock cubes onion, curry powder, all purpose seasoning, thyme, garlic powder, ½ tsp chilli powder
    o Add 200mls of water
    o Cover askew and cook at medium heat for 20 minutes (30 minutes if tough meat is used) stirring from time to time
- Preheat the oven to 170°C/350°F/gas 4

Step 2:
- Blend:
    o Tin tomato, tomato puree, ½ tsp chilli powder, onion, red pepper, scotch bonnet and 100mls of water

Step 3:
- Line the baking tray with foil and grease with a little bit of oil
- Strain the meat/chicken once boiled, keeping aside the stock and place them straight onto the baking tray
- Drizzle some stock and oil on top
- Roast the meat/chicken in oven for 30 minutes until golden, turning half-way through

Step 4:
- Heat the oil in medium saucepan for 3 minutes on medium heat
- Add blended mix which should sizzle if the oils is hot enough
- Add 1 chicken stock cube and 2 Maggi stock cubes cover and cook for 5 minutes
- Add the roasted meat and stir in
- Cook covered for 20 minutes, stirring regularly
- Add some sieved stock from boiled meat and cook for further 10 minutes

Serving Suggestions
Ideally serve with Rice, Amala, Yam, Dodo or bread. Try a little bit of stew with almost anything, potatoes (including mashed), chips, fish or eggs.

Ila

Serves 4-6

Ingredients:
- 23 Okra
- 750mls Water
- 1 Maggi stock cube
- ¼ tsp Salt

Equipment:
- Measuring jug
- Food blender
- Medium saucepan

Cooking guide:

Steps:
- Boil the water in the saucepan, along with salt and crushed Maggie
- Chop the ends off the Okra and discard them, then chop what is left into thirds
- Blend using the pulsed option on the blender*, if available
- Once blended add the okra to the boiling water and stir in thoroughly
- Cook uncovered on medium heat for 5 minutes, stirring regularly
- Be watchful as it has a tendency to bubble up and spill, especially if covered

*Traditionally the okra should be sliced down the middle diagonally and chopped into 0.5cm pieces for the really authentic preparation. However, for convenience a blender works.

Serving Suggestions

Ideal with Iyan, Amala, Eba, Ground Rice and topped with Obe Ata and meat/chicken.

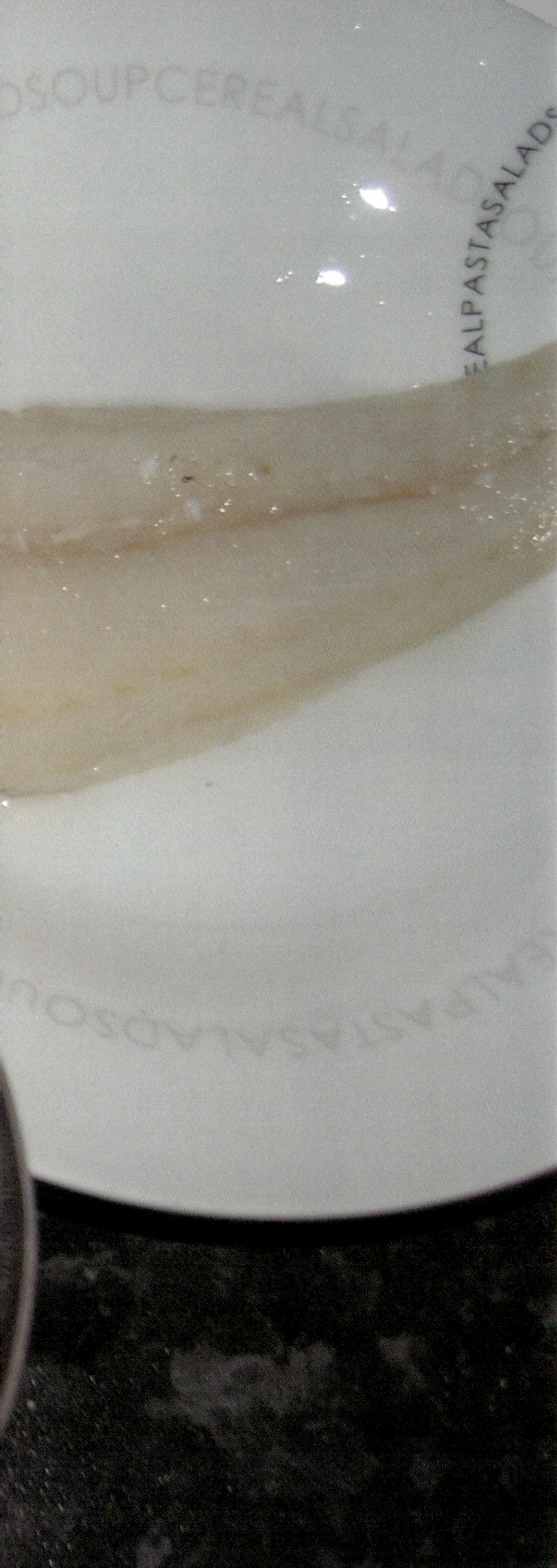

Ogbono

Serves 6-8

Ingredients:

- 500g diced Meat/Chicken
- ½ tsp Mild curry powder
- 1/8 tsp Garlic powder
- ½ tsp Chilli powder (optional)
- ½ tsp All purpose seasoning
- 150g Fresh or smoked fish
- 250mls Palm oil
- ½ cup Ground Ogbono
- 1 tbsp Locust beans
- 400g Tin of plum tomato
- 1 Medium onion
- 1 Medium red pepper
- ½-2 Scotch bonnet
- 550mls Water
- 1 Chicken and 3 Maggi stock cubes

Equipment:

- Food blender/mill
- Large saucepan
- Measuring jug
- Stirring spoon
- Slotted spoon

Cooking guide:

Step 1:
- Blend:
  - Tin tomato, onion, red pepper, scotch bonnet and 100mls of cold water

Step 2:
- Rinse and dice the meat/chicken of your choice
- Place all the meat into a saucepan and add 1 Maggi, curry powder, all purpose seasoning and garlic powder with 150mls of cold water
- Boil the meat for 15 minutes

Step 3:
- Mill the Ogbono if the non-powdered form has been bought.

Step 4:

- Heat the palm oil (in its container) in the microwave to loosen it for 30 seconds
- Heat 250mls of palm oil in the saucepan for 2 minutes
- Add the powdered Ogbono gradually to the oil stirring continuously to avoid lumps
- Stir, cover askew and boil for 5 minutes

Step 5:

- Add the blended mix, crush in the 1 chicken and 2 Maggi stock cubes, and 300mls of cold water
- Cover and cook for further 10 minutes

Step 6:

- Add the final ingredients of locust beans, meat/chicken and fish cover and cook for 10 minutes

Serving Suggestions

Enjoy with either Iyan, Amala or Ground rice. Topping with Obe Ata in this case is optional.

Efo Riro

Serves 4-6

Ingredients:
- 300g Spinach
- 2 Cod fillets
- 400g Tin plum tomato
- 1 Medium onion
- 1 Red pepper
- ½ - 3 Scotch bonnet
- 300mls Water
- 1 Chicken, 1 Maggi stock cubes
- 1 tsp Mild curry powder
- 1 tsp All purpose seasoning
- 1 tsp Thyme
- ½ tsp Garlic powder
- 1-2 tsp Chilli powder (optional)
- 200mls Palm oil
- ½ tsp Salt

Equipment:
- 1 Medium saucepan
- Food blender
- Stirring spoon
- Colander
- Measuring jug

Cooking guide:

Step 1:
- Blend:
  - Tin tomato, onion, red pepper, scotch bonnet, chilli powder and 100mls of water

Step 2:
- Rinse spinach under cold water
- Place in saucepan with 200mls cold water and simmer on low for 7 minutes
- Drain excess water and leave in colander

Step 3:
- If using frozen fish will need to allow to thaw for 3 hours before use
- Rinse the cod fillets
- Cut the cod fillets into 1 ½ cm strips and place aside

Step 4:
- Heat palm oil with bottle for 30 seconds in the microwave
- Heat palm oil for 3 minutes in a medium pan on medium heat
- Add the blended mix from step 1 once oil is heated
- Crush and add the chicken and Maggi stock cubes
- Add the curry powder, all purpose seasoning, thyme and garlic powder
- Add the fish
- Stir, cover askew and cook for 15 minutes

Step 5:
- Stir mixture
- Add spinach
- Add salt and stir in, cover and cook for further 7-10 minutes stirring regularly

Serving Suggestions

Enjoy hot with either Iyan, Ground rice, Amala or Eba. Add Obe Ata on top with meat/chicken.

Efo with Egusi

Serves 4-6

Ingredients:

- 350g Spinach
- 2 Cod fillets
- 400g Tin plum tomato
- 1 Medium onion
- 1 Medium red pepper
- ½ - 3 Scotch bonnet
- 1 Chicken and 2 Maggi stock cubes
- 1 ½ tsp Mild curry powder
- 1 tsp All purpose seasoning
- 1 tsp Thyme
- ½ tsp Garlic powder
- 2 tsp Chilli powder (optional)
- 100mls Palm oil
- 1 cup Ground egusi
- 1 cup Ground crayfish (optional)
- 1 tbsp Locust beans (optional)
- 600mls Water
- ½ tsp Salt

Equipment:

- 2 Medium saucepans
- Food blender/mill
- Medium bowl
- Stirring spoon
- Colander

Whole Crayfish

Cooking guide:

Step 1:
- Blend:
  - Tin tomato, onion, red pepper, scotch bonnet, chilli powder and 100mls of water

Step 2:
- Rinse spinach under cold water
- Place in saucepan with 200mls cold water and simmer for 7 minutes
- Drain excess water and leave in colander
- Mill the crayfish, if bought whole as in the picture above

Step 3:
- Place ground egusi into a bowl
- Mix in 75mls of cold water until paste-like

Step 4:
- If using frozen fish will need to allow to thaw for 3 hours before use
- Rinse the cod fillets
- Cut the cod fillets into 1 ½ cm strips and place aside

Step 5:
- Heat the palm oil bottle in the microwave for 30 seconds
- Place palm oil in the saucepan, on medium heat for 3 minutes
- Place balls of egusi into the hot palm oil
- Allow to fry in oil for 3 minutes not stirring

Step 6:

- Add blended mix from step 1 to the saucepan
- Add 225mls of cold water
- Add the milled crayfish and stir in
- Add chicken and Maggi stock cubes, curry powder, all purpose seasoning, garlic powder, chilli powder, thyme and fish
- Mix in above, including lifting the egusi from the bottom of the saucepan and cover to cook for 25 minutes stirring it regularly

Step 7:

- Stir in the locust beans and the spinach
- Add salt and stir in, cover and cook for further 7-10 minutes stirring regularly

Serving Suggestions

Serve hot with either Iyan, Ground rice, Amala or Eba. Top with Obe Ata meat/chicken.

Ewedu

Serves 4-6

Ingredients:
- 300g of Ewedu leaves
- 1 tsp Locust beans
- Small pinch of Potash (optional)
- 1 Maggi stock cube
- 500mls Water

Equipment:
- Small saucepan
- Stirring spoon
- Measuring jug
- Metal whisk

Cooking guide:

Step 1:
- Place the water in the saucepan with potash and bring to the boil
- Add the Maggi stock cube

Step 2:
- Rinse the Ewedu and add it to the boiling water
- Add the locust beans
- Stir in and cover askew
- Cook for 20 minutes, on medium heat stirring regularly

Step 3:
- Take the Ewedu off the heat and slowly whisk the soup to break up the leaves

Serving Suggestions
Serve hot with either Iyan, Ground rice, Amala or Eba. Top with Obe Ata and meat/chicken.

Gbegiri

Serves 4-6

Ingredients:
- 200g Peeled black-eyed beans
- ½ Red pepper
- 1 Large onion
- ½ - 2 Scotch Bonnet
- 1 Chicken and 1 Maggi stock cubes
- ½ tsp Salt
- 125mls Palm oil
- 600mls Water

Equipment:
- Food blender
- Medium saucepan
- Mixing spoon
- Measuring jug

Cooking guide:

Step 1:
- Rinse the beans and place in the saucepan with 200mls of water
- Slice onion and red pepper, along with whole scotch bonnet into the saucepan
- Boil for 30 minutes on medium heat

Step 2:
- Remove from the heat and allow to cool down

Step 3:
- Blend all the cooled mixture into liquid adding 50mls of water with each blend

Step 4:
- Add the blended mixture to the saucepan
- Add 200mls of water
- Add chicken and Maggi stock cubes and salt
- Stir in well, cover askew and cook on medium heat for 20 minutes, stirring intermittently

Step 5:
- Heat the palm oil bottle in the microwave for 30 seconds
- Add the palm oil to the saucepan and stir in
- Cover askew and cook for a further 15 minutes

Serving Suggestions
Serve hot with Amala, Iyan, Eba or Ground rice. Top with Obe Ata and meat/ chicken.

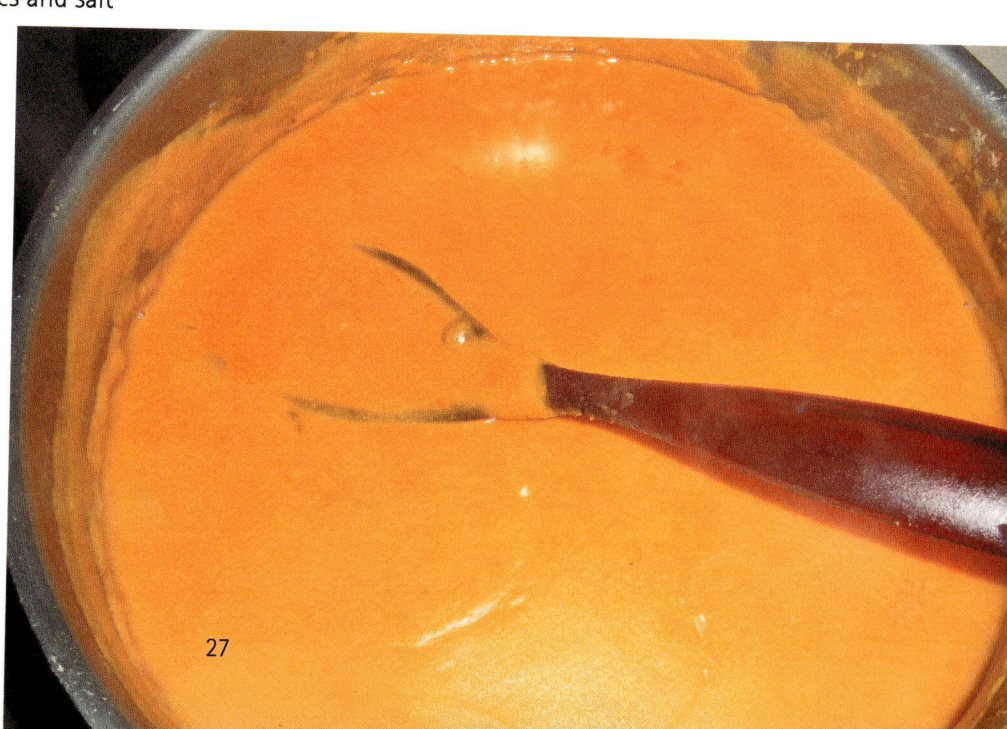

Rice and Staples

Plain white rice served with Boli and Obe Ata

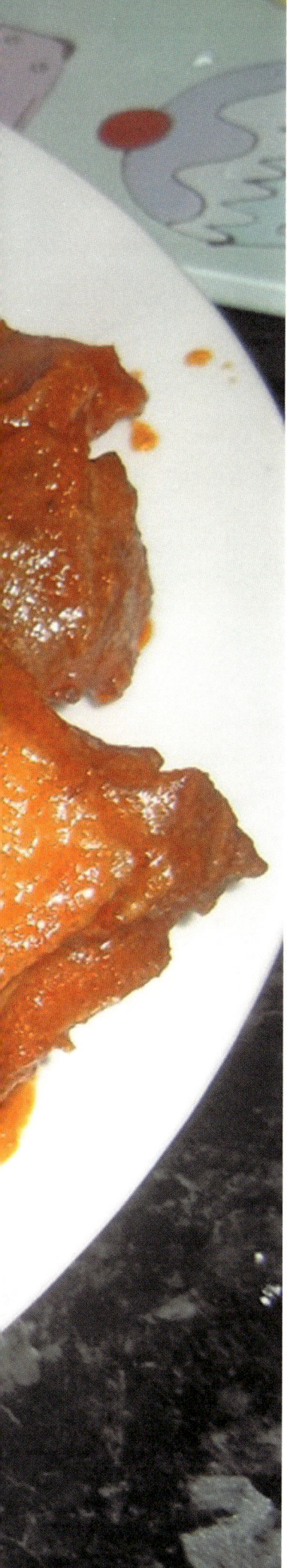

Plain White Rice

Serves 4-6

Ingredients:
- 2 cups Easy cook long grain white rice
- 900mls Cold water
- ½ - 1 tsp Salt
- 1 ½ cups of mixed vegetables

Equipment:
- Medium & small saucepans
- Stirring spoon
- Measuring jug and cups
- Colander

Cooking guide:

Step1:
- Add 2 cups of rice to a medium saucepan
- Add 350mls of cold water
- Cover askew and boil for 7 minutes on medium heat
- Take the rice off the heat and rinse under cold water until water from the rice is clear
- Place back on the stove with 350mls of water
- Add salt and stir
- Cover askew and cook for 10 minutes, checking regularly
- The rice is ready when it is soft but not mushy

Step 2:
- Place 1 ½ cups of frozen mixed vegetables in a small saucepan
- Add 200mls of water, cover askew and simmer for 5 minutes
- Once ready drain off the excess water through the colander

Serving Suggestions
To be eaten with Obe Ata meat/chicken; adding Dodo or Boli and Moin-moin if desired.

Fried Rice

Serves 4-6

Ingredients:
- 1 ½ cups Easy cook long grain white rice
- 1 Chicken and 1 Maggi stock cubes
- ¼ tsp Turmeric
- ¼ tsp Salt
- 1/8 tsp Garlic powder
- ¼ tsp All purpose seasoning
- ¼ tsp Mild curry powder
- 2 cups Frozen mixed vegetables
- 2 Eggs
- 50mls Vegetable/Sunflower oil
- 700mls Water
- 30mls Semi-skimmed milk

Equipment:
- Large, medium & small saucepans
- Small frying saucepan
- Mixing spoon
- 2 Medium mixing bowls
- Metal whisk
- Measuring jug & cups
- Colander

Cooking guide:

Step 1:
- Boil rice in 350mls of water for 7 ½ minutes in a medium saucepan on medium heat covered askew
- Remove the rice from the stove and rinse thoroughly in cold water, repeatedly until water is clear
- Drain off any extra water and place the rice to one side in a mixing bowl

Step 2:
- Place the saucepan with 600mls of cold water on the cooker on medium heat
- Crush ¾ chicken and 1 Maggi stock cubes into the water
- Add garlic powder, turmeric, all purpose seasoning, curry powder
- Cover and boil for 10 minutes

Step 3:
- Add the rice to the boiling seasoned water and stir in thoroughly
- Cover askew and cook for 15 minutes

Step 4:
- Place 2 cups of frozen mixed vegetables in a small saucepan on medium heat
- Add 1/8 tsp salt and ¼ chicken stock cube
- Boil for 7 minutes
- Drain and place aside

Step 5:
- Crack 2 eggs into a bowl
- Add 30mls of semi-skimmed milk and 1/8 tsp of salt
- Whisk the eggs gently
- Heat 20mls of vegetable oil in a small frying pan
- Add egg and scramble

Step 6:
- Heat 30mls of vegetable oil in a large pan on medium heat for 2 minutes
- Add mixed vegetables and pan-fry for 2 minutes
- Stir in scrambled egg for 1 minute
- Add rice and mix in well and cook for further 4 minutes

Serving Suggestions
Serve with Roasted or fried meat/chicken, Suya or Obe Ata and chicken/meat. Additionally this dish can be enjoyed with Moin-moin and Dodo or Boli.

Jollof Rice

Serves 4-6

Ingredients:

- 2 cups Easy cook long grain rice
- 200g Tin plum tomato
- Large onion
- ½ Medium red pepper
- ½-2 Scotch bonnet
- 2 cups Frozen mixed vegetables
- 50mls Water
- 170g Corned beef
- 1 Chicken and 2 Maggi stock cubes
- 100mls Vegetable/Sunflower oil
- 1 Large egg
- ¼ tsp Garlic powder
- ½ tsp All purpose seasoning
- ½ tsp Mild curry powder
- ½ tsp Thyme

Equipment:

- Food blender
- Large & medium saucepans
- Stirring spoon
- Colander

Cooking guide:

Step 1:
- Blend:
  o Tin tomato, onion, red pepper, scotch bonnet and 50mls of water

Step 2:
- Heat vegetable oil in a large saucepan for 2 minutes on medium heat
- Add the blended mix to the oil
- Stir in garlic powder, all purpose seasoning, curry powder and thyme
- Cover askew and allow to boil for 15 minutes

Step 3:
- Meanwhile add 2 cups of rice to the medium saucepan
- Add 350mls of cold water
- Cover askew and allow to boil for 7 minutes on medium heat
- Take the rice off the heat and rinse under cold water until water is clear

Step 4:
- Rinse the mixed vegetables
- Add the rinsed mixed vegetables, egg and crushed corned beef to the blended mix
- Stir thoroughly and allow to cook, covered askew for 5 minutes
- Add the part-boiled rice and stir in all ingredients
- Cover and cook for 10 minutes on medium heat, gently turning regularly

Serving Suggestions
Serve with Roasted/Fried meat, Suya or Obe Ata and meat/chicken. This dish can also be enjoyed with Dodo or Boli and Moin-moin.

Iyan

Obe Ata

Efo Riro

Iyan

Serves 4-6

Ingredients:
- 6 cups Pounded yam
- 3L Water

Equipment:
- Medium saucepan
- Orogun
- Igbako
- Measuring jug

Cooking Guide:

Step 1:
- Bring the water to boil in the saucepan on medium heat

Step 2:
- Decant half of the boiled water into the measuring jug
- Reduce the cooker heat to low
- Add the pounded yam flour to the water all at once
- Allow it to sit for about 30 seconds, then pound the flour and water in together using the Orogun
- After 1 minute of pounding, turn the heat back up to medium
- Once the mixture becomes more dough-like, pound it against the side of the saucepan

Step 3:
- Stop mixing
- Add the water previously removed to bath the Iyan
- Cover askew and allow to simmer for 5 minutes
- Drain any excess water away
- Pound the mixture again until all the water has dried up

Step 4:
- Wet, ever so slightly, all the plates before serving the Iyan in order that it doesn't stick too much to the plates
- Serve into individual portions using the Igbako

Serving Suggestions
This should be eaten relatively soon after making to enjoy it best. Serve with Gbegiri, Efo Riro, Egusi or Okra. Top with Obe Ata and meat.

Please note that there is a further type of staple called Ground rice. Now for the instructions on how to prepare this, follow the instructions for making Iyan, adjusting only in step 2. At this point instead of pouring all the Ground rice into the hot water at once, you put it in mixing it continuously as you do so. Ground rice is to be served and eaten with the same soups and Obe Ata as mentioned above.

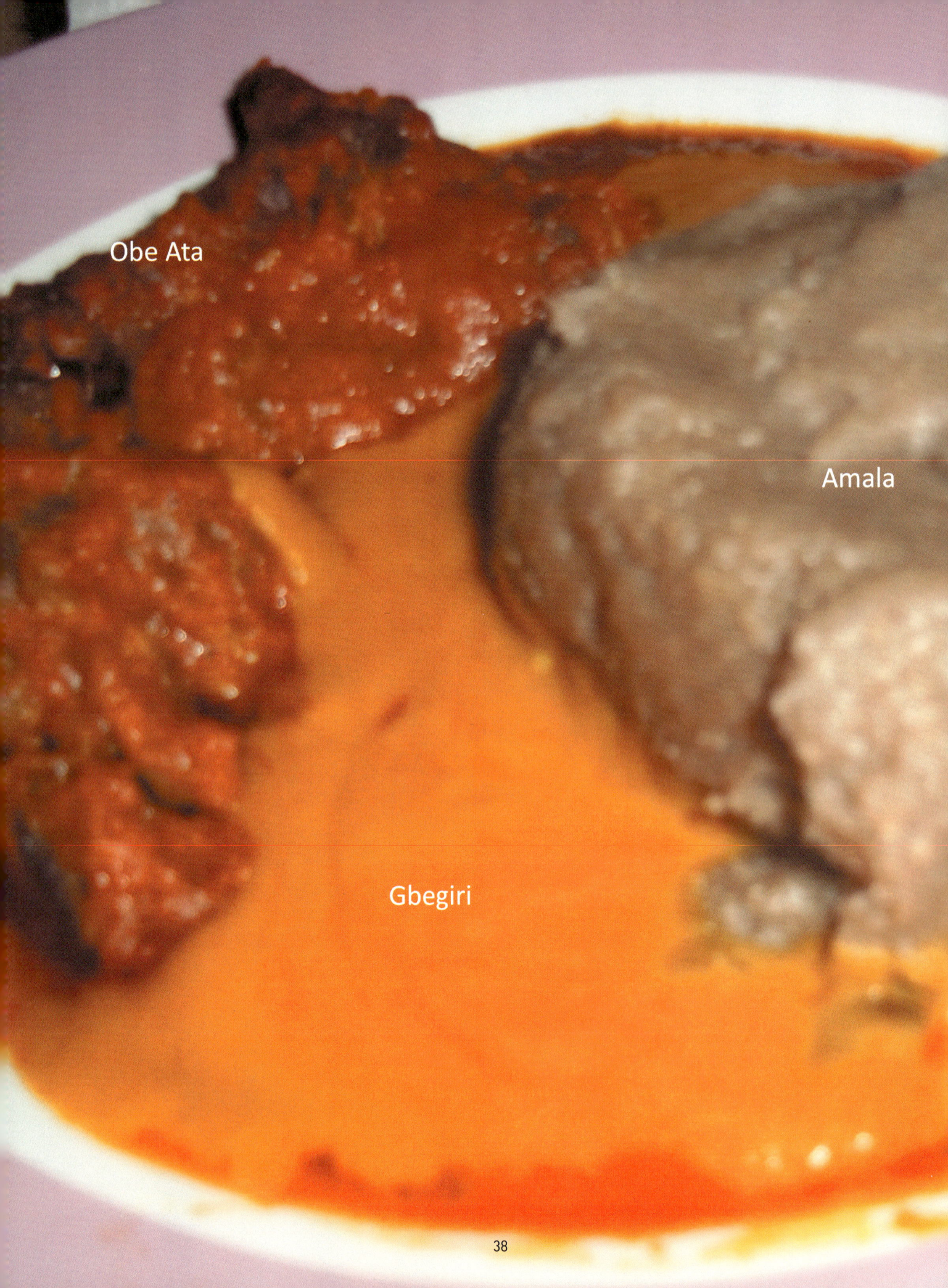

Obe Ata

Amala

Gbegiri

Amala

Serves 4-6

Ingredients:
- 6 cups Elubo
- 3.5l Water

Equipment:
- Medium saucepan
- Orogun
- Igbako
- Measuring jug

Cooking Guide:

Step 1:
- Boil water in saucepan on medium heat

Step 2:
- Decant half the water into the measuring jug
- Reduce the heat to low
- Add the Elubo to the water all at once
- Allow to sit for about 30 seconds, then pound the Elubo and water in together
- After 1 minute, turn the heat back up to medium
- Once the mixture becomes more dough-like, pound it against the side of the saucepan

Step 3:
- Stop mixing
- Add the water previously removed to bath the Elubo
- Cover and allow to simmer for 5 minutes
- Drain any excess water away
- Pound the mixture again until all the water has dried up

Step 4:
- Wet, ever so slightly, all the plates before serving the Iyan in order that it doesn't stick too much to the plates
- Serve into individual portions using the Igbako

Serving Suggestions
This is best eaten as soon as it's made. Serve with either Gbegiri, Efo, Egusi or Okra. Top with Obe Ata and meat/chicken.

Eba

Serves 4-6

Ingredients:
- 6 cups Gari
- 2.2l Boiled water

Equipment:
- Medium saucepan
- Orogun
- Igbako
- Measuring jug

Cooking Guide:

Step 1:
- Boil the water then turn off the heat (or boil the water in the kettle)
- Keep 1/3 aside in a measuring jug

Step 2:
- Add the Gari until all the water is absorbed
- Leave it to stand for 2 minutes
- Using the Orogun in a pounding type motion, pound until dough-like

Step 3:
- Add the remaining 1/3 cups of water to bath the eba for 3 minutes
- Drain off any extra water
- Now pound the Eba again until smooth (but still with a dough-like consistency)

Serving suggestions
Serve with Efo, Egusi or Ogbono, topping with Obe Ata and meat/chicken.

Ewa

Serves 6-8

Ingredients:

- 2 cups Nigerian beans
- 180mls Palm oil
- 400g Tin chopped tomato
- 1 Large onion
- Fish e.g 185g of Tuna can
- 3 Maggi stock cubes
- ½ tsp Salt
- ½ - 2 Scotch bonnet
- 1 tsp Chilli powder
- 500mls Water

Equipment:

- Large & small saucepan
- Pressure cooker (preferred)
- Stirring spoon
- Tin opener
- 1 Medium bowl
- Potato masher

Cooking guide:

Step 1:

- Place beans on flat surface and pick out any impurities
- Place in bowl with 1L of boiled water and allow to soak for 24 hours before use to allow to soften
- Then boil the beans with plenty of water until soft, adding more water as is required, this may take several hours
- If you have a pressure cooker then place the beans in the cooker and follow the cooker's instruction (usually the beans will take about 45-60 minutes to cook)

Step 2:

- Heat palm oil bottle in microwave for 30 seconds
- Poor the palm oil in large saucepan and heat for 2 minutes on medium heat
- Add the chopped: tomato, onion, scotch bonnets
- Crush in 2 Maggi stock cubes adding along side the chilli powder and 300mls of water
- Stir and cook covered askew on medium heat, stirring regularly for 15 minutes
- Now add your choice of fish
- Cover and cook for further 15 minutes on low heat

Step 3:

- Drain excess water off from the beans
- Add the palm oil mix to the beans and stir in well
- Cover and cook for a further 10 minutes
- Mash and cook covered askew for a further 2 minutes

Serving Suggestions
Eat alone or with Dodo, Boli, Gari, Roasted/Fried meat/chicken.

Isu

Serves 4-6

Ingredients:
- 1 Medium Punna yam
- ½ tsp Salt
- ½ tsp Sugar (optional)
- Water

Equipment:
- Chopping board
- Chopping knife
- Large saucepan
- Slotted spoon

Cooking guide:

Step 1:
- Place the yam on the chopping board
- Cut the ends off the yam and discard them
- Cut the yam into pieces that are roughly 2cm wide
- Peel the skin off all the yam pieces. Easiest way to do this is to place each of the yam slices flat on the chopping board and calve off the skin, taking off as little yam as possible.

Step 2:
- Rinse the yam pieces and place them in the saucepan
- Add the salt (and sugar)
- Fill the pan with enough water to cover the yam
- Cover askew and boil for 40 minutes, be watchful as you may need to add more water

Step 3:
- Once boiled remove the yam from any excess water with the slotted spoon into the colander
- Leave to stand for 2 minutes

Serving Suggestions
Serve with Eyin Dindin, mixed vegetables and Obe Ata. This dish can also be enjoyed with Ewa.

Isu Dindin

Serves 4 - 6

Ingredients:
- 1 Medium Punna yam
- 1 ½ tsp Salt
- ½ tsp Sugar (optional)
- 350mls Vegetable/Sunflower oil

Equipment:
- Chopping board and knife
- Colander
- Frying pan
- Slotted spoon

Cooking guide:

Step 1:
- Cut the ends off the yam and throw them away
- Cut the yam into pieces that are roughly 2cm wide
- Peel the skin off all the yam pieces. Again here the easiest way to do this is to place each of the yam slices flat on the chopping board and calve off the skin, taking off as little yam as possible.
- Then dice each slice into 4 pieces

Step 2:
- Rinse the yam pieces and place them in the colander
- Add the salt (and sugar)

Step 3:
- Heat oil in frying pan on medium heat for 3 minutes
- Place pieces of yam into the oil
- Fry the pieces for 25 minutes turning regularly so golden on all sides
- Repeat the process until all the pieces are done

Serving Suggestions
Serve with Eyin Dindin and Obe Ata. You can add some Dodo to this dish also if you desire.

Asaro

Serves 6-8

Ingredients:
- 1medium Punna yam
- 400g tin Chopped tomato
- 1 Large onion
- 1 Red pepper
- 3 Fillets of cod
- 10mls Puree
- 120mls Palm oil
- ½ - 2 Scotch bonnet
- 1 Chicken and 2 Maggi stock cubes
- 1 tsp Chilli powder
- 1 tsp Salt
- Water

Equipment:
- Chopping board and knife
- Food blender
- Large saucepan
- Stirring spoon
- Colander
- Potato masher

Cooking guide:

Step 1:
- Slice yam into roughly 1 inch slices
- Peel off skin and rinse. Easiest way to do this is to place each of the yam slices flat on the chopping board and calve off the skin, taking off as little yam as possible.
- Once peeled, cut yam slices into 4

Step 2:
- Place yam into saucepan and half fill with water and add salt
- Boil yam for 20 minutes on medium heat
- Once underway with step 1 start on steps 2 and 3
- Once cooked place the yam pieces in the colander

Step 3:
- Blend:
  - Tin tomato, onion, red pepper, scotch bonnet, puree, chilli powder and 100mls of water

Step 4:
- Heat palm oil in microwave for 30 seconds
- Decant the palm oil into the saucepan on medium heat
- Add the blended mix to the saucepan
- Crush and add the chicken and Maggi stock cubes and stir in
- Cover askew, and cook for 15 minutes, stirring regularly

Step 5:
- Now add the yam, fish and salt
- Mix well, cover askew and cook for further 12 minutes
- Mash the ingredients together and cook for further 3 minutes

Serving Suggestions
Eat with either Roasted or Fried meat/chicken. Why not top with some Obe Ata?

Side Dishes

Ogi

Serves 4-6

Ingredients:
- 175g Ogi powder
- 4tsp Sugar (optional)
- 50mls Evaporated milk
- 900mls Water (200mls lukewarm, 700mls boiling)

Equipment:
- Medium saucepan
- Wooden spoon

Cooking guide:

Step 1:
- Boil 700mls of water

Step 2:
- Pour Ogi powder into the saucepan
- Mix in 200mls of lukewarm water to form a custard thick fluid

Step 3:
- Gradually stir in the boiled water until you reach an even consistency
- Add the sugar and stir in thoroughly

Step 4:
- Place saucepan on low heat for 3-5 minutes, stirring occasionally

Step 5:
- Pour 10mls of cold water into bowls before serving the Ogi
- Add extra sugar, if desired and milk to taste

Serving Suggestions
This dish is eaten mostly at breakfast time and is usually served with Akara or Moin-moin.

Ojojo

Serves 6-8

Ingredients:
- ½ Medium Punna yam
- 1 Medium onion
- 125g Small shrimps
- 1 tsp Chilli powder
- 1 tsp Salt
- 350mls Vegetable/Sunflower oil

Equipment:
- Chopping board
- Chopping knife
- Metal grater
- Slotted spoon
- Colander
- Mixing bowl
- Frying pan

Cooking guide:

Step 1:
- Chop, peel and grate the yam into the bowl. Still the easiest way to do this is to place each of the yam slices flat on the chopping board and calve off the skin, taking off as little yam as possible.
- <u>DO NOT RINSE!</u>
- Grate the onion and add to the yam
- Add the shrimp, but squeeze first to remove as much excess water as possible
- Add salt and chilli to taste
- Thoroughly mix all ingredients together

Step 2:
- Heat oil in frying pan on medium heat
- Place handfuls of the mixture in the oil and deep fry
- Allow to cook for 2 minutes and turn over with the slotted spoon
- Continue to turnover until each side is golden brown
- Remove and place in the colander
- Continue process until all the mixture is finished

Serving Suggestions
Eat while hot as a snack alone or as part of a meal with Eyin Dindin, Obe Ata.

Akara

Serves 6-8

Ingredients:
- 500g Peeled black-eyed beans
- 1 Red pepper
- ½ - 2 Scotch bonnet
- 1 Large onion
- 2 tsp Powdered stock
- 1 tsp Salt
- 500mls Vegetable oil
- 1.2l Boiled water

Equipment:
- Large bowl
- Stirring spoon
- Slotted spoon
- Medium frying pan
- Colander
- Food blender
- Ladle

Cooking guide:

Step 1:
- Soak peeled beans in boiled water (1.2l) for at least 2 hours

Step 2: *
- Drain excess water from the beans using the colander
- Add chopped red pepper, onion and scotch bonnet
- Blend the above together (in portions that fill the blender ¼ full) adding 50mls of water, each time until it is fluid (mixture should be thick)
- Once all blended add the powdered stock and salt having dissolved them in a little hot water
- Stir in all ingredients with the stirring spoon

Step 3:
- Heat oil in frying pan, on medium heat for 3 minutes (needs to be deep)
- Add Scooped ladles of the mixture to the oil, giving separate equal-sized portions
- Fry on 1 side until mixture starts to float then flip them over using the slotted spoon
- Once golden-orange in colour remove, placing in the colander and turn down heat
- Repeat the steps above turning the heat back up to medium once the mixture is added

*Step 2: Modified version would be to use the beans flour. Blend all the other ingredients and pour into a large bowl. Add the beans flour stirring in continuously to avoid lumps until the mixture is thick and a spoonful of it will sit on top of the rest of the mixture. Leave to set for 2 hours. Resume instructions at step 3.

Serving Suggestions
Once cooked eat with Ogi, Gari, bread or alone as a tasty snack.

Moin-moin

Serves 6-8

Ingredients:
- 400g Peeled black-eyed beans
- 1 Large red pepper
- 1 Large onion
- ½ - 3 Scotch bonnets
- 1.2L Water: 600mls cold and 600mls boiled
- 4 Large boiled eggs
- 50mls Vegetable/Sunflower oil
- 1 Chicken and 2 Maggi stock cubes
- 1 tsp Salt
- 340g Corned-beef

Equipment:
- 6 Tin foil containers with lids
- 1 Large saucepan/2 medium saucepan
- Food blender
- 1 Large bowl
- Newspaper
- Ladle
- Egg slicer

Cooking guide:

Step 1:
- Soak peeled beans in water (1.2L) for at least 1 hour
- Chop up the corned beef
- Boil 4 eggs, cool and slice

Step 2:
- Drain excess water from the beans
- Add chopped red pepper, onion and scotch bonnet
- blend above (in portions that fill the blender 1/3 full) with 70mls of water, each time until it's fluid
- Once all blended add the chicken and Maggi stock cubes and salt, having dissolved them in hot water beforehand

Step 3:
- Heat oil for 1 minute in the microwave
- Add and stir into the blended beans

Step 4:
- Take 16 oz foil containers and half fill with blended mixture
- Add some corned beef and egg slices
- Fill container with more blended mixture
- Cover with lid (foil side down)
- Repeat the above process until all mixture used

Step 4:
- Fill saucepan 1/3 full with cold water (1 large saucepan or 2 medium saucepans)
- Place filled foil containers in saucepan, stacked unevenly, but all upright
- Add 3 little knots of newspaper into the water in the saucepan
- Cover with newspaper, folded to the circumference of the saucepan
- Cover the saucepan and boil for 45 minutes on medium heat, checking regularly that there is enough water

Serving Suggestions
This can be enjoyed alone or with any of the Rice dishes, Roasted or Fried meat/chicken, Dodo, Boli or Gari. This dish is lovely garnished with Obe Ata.

Dodo

Serves 4-6

Ingredients:
- 2 large Yellow plantains
- 400mls Vegetable/Sunflower oil
- ¼ tsp Salt

Equipment:
- Frying pan
- Slotted spoon
- Colander

Cooking guide:

Step 1:
- Peel the plantain
- Chop plantain into cubes, slices or half-slices into the colander
- Add salt and shake to spread the salt around

Step 2:
- Heat oil for 3 minutes on medium heat
- Add plantain and allow to fry turning over once brown on one side with the slotted spoon
- After about 15 minutes, remove and place in colander

Serving Suggestions
Serve with any of the Rice dishes, Ewa or Isu. Why not top with Obe Ata and meat/chicken? You can also try Dodo as a snack alone hot or cold.

Boli

Serves 4-6

Ingredients:
- 2 large Yellow plantains
- 20mls Vegetable/Sunflower oil
- ¼ tsp Salt

Equipment:
- Baking tray
- Chopping knife
- Kitchen foil

Cooking guide:

Step 1:
- Preheat the oven on 150°C/300°F/gas 3

Step 2:
- Peel the plantain
- Garnish with salt and drizzle the oil all over

Step 3:
- Line the baking tray with kitchen foil
- Place plantains on baking tray
- Allow to brown on one side for 15 minutes
- Turn and bake on the other side for a further 10 minutes

Serving Suggestions
Serve with any of the Rice dishes, Ewa or Isu; top with Obe Ata . Why not try it as a snack alone hot or cold?

Eyin Dindin

Serves 4-6

Ingredients:
- 6 Eggs
- ½ Chicken and 1 Maggi stock cubes
- 1 Can sardines (optional)
- ½ - 2 Scotch bonnet
- ½ tsp Chilli powder
- 40mls Vegetable/Sunflower oil
- ¼ tsp Salt
- 1 Small onion
- 1 Fresh tomato
- 10mls Tomato puree

Equipment:
- Medium frying pan
- Medium bowl
- Slotted spoon
- Metal whisk

Cooking guide:

Step 1:
- Heat 40mls of oil in frying pan on medium heat
- Chop the onion, tomato and scotch bonnet
- Add chopped mix to frying pan and stir in
- After 5 minutes add chicken and Maggi stock cube, chilli powder and puree, stirring in
- Leave to sizzle for further 2 minutes

Step 2:
- Crack and whisk 6 egg in a bowl
- Add salt and whisk some more

Step 3:
- Add eggs to frying pan and mix in with the slotted spoon
- Stir from time to so that mixture does not burn
- Within 5 minutes the egg should be ready

Serving Suggestions
Enjoy this with either Isu, potato, bread or Dodo. This goes very well with chips too!

Snacks

Meat Pies

Serves 6-8

Ingredients:

Dough
- 4 ¼ Cups of plain flour
- 4 Medium eggs
- 1 ½ tsp Salt
- 150g Butter
- ¾ Cup of semi-skimmed milk

Filling
- 800g Diced beef
- 2 Medium potatoes
- 4 Maggi stock cubes
- ¼ tsp Garlic powder
- ¼ tsp All purpose seasoning
- 1/8 tsp Curry powder
- 1 tsp Chilli powder
- 1 tsp Salt

Equipment:
- Oven
- Large saucepan
- Stirring spoon
- 2 Baking trays
- Colander
- Large bowl
- Sieve
- Chopping board
- Rolling pin
- 7cm pastry cutters
- Metal whisk

Cooking guide:

Step 1:
- Preheat the oven 170°C/350°F/gas 4

Step 2:
- Dice the beef, rinse and place in saucepan
- Boil the beef with garlic powder, all purpose seasoning, curry powder, chilli and salt for 12 minutes on medium heat, covered askew
- Stir occasionally

Step 3:
- Dice and rinse potatoes
- Add potatoes to boiling beef and cook together for a further 10 minutes

Step 4:
- Empty the beef/potato combination into a colander to cool

Step 5:
- Sieve flour into large bowl
- Melt butter and add 3 eggs, whisking together
- Add butter/eggs to flour
- Add milk
- Knead mixture together until smooth – add more

flour to create dough

Step 6:
- Roll out the dough on flour-dusted chopping board
- Use pastry cutter to section the dough
- Fill pouch with beef/potato mix
- Fold over the pastry so the ends meet at the top and place aside
- Repeat step 6 until all the dough and meat is finished

Step 7:
- Lightly oil the baking tray
- Using the pastry brush garnish each pastry with egg yolk and place on the baking tray
- Bake in oven for about 30 minutes

Serving Suggestions

Allow to cool and eat as tasty snack with the beverage of your choice.

68

Suya

Serves 6-8

Ingredients:
- 1Kg Diced beef
- 1 tbsp Chilli powder
- 2 tsp Salt
- 2 Sliced tomatoes
- 1 Large sliced onion
- 250g Ground peanut (unsalted)
- 1 Palm-sized portion of ginger
- 1 ½ Garlic
- 2 tsp Paprika
- 1 Red and 1 green pepper
- 2½ tbsp Vegetable/Sunflower oil

Equipment:
- Large mixing bowl
- Baking trays
- Wooden spoon
- Large skewers
- Medium saucepan
- BBQ/Oven
- Kitchen foil
- Mill

Cooking guide:

Step 1:
- Preheat oven, if using this to cook Suya, to 170°C/350°F/gas 4

Step 2:
- Boil:
  - Rinse the pieces of beef in cold water and place in the medium saucepan
  - Add the 1 chicken and 3 Maggi stock cubes onion, ½ tsp chilli powder
  - Add 200mls of water
  - Cover askew and cook at medium heat for 10 minutes stirring from time to time
- Remove meat into a colander and allow to cool

Step 3:
- Chop and grind the garlic and ginger
- Mix the ½ tsp oil, ground peanuts, paprika, chilli powder, salt, garlic and ginger until paste like

Step 4:
- Chop the onions, tomato and peppers into small strips

Step 5:
- Place the beef from step 2 into the mix
- Ensure all the beef is as covered as possible

Step 6:
- Fill the skewers with beef and chopped vegetables from step 4
- Repeat this step until all the beef and vegetables are used up
- If using an oven lightly douse the meat with some oil to prevent over drying

Step 7:
- Ideally the skewers would be cooked on a BBQ or on a charcoal fire for 10-15 minutes turning frequently until evenly roasted
- In the absence of coal fire use an oven for 30 minutes
- Turn skewers over after 15 minutes to ensure browning evenly on all sides

Serving Suggestions
Eat hot or cold served as a snack or starter. It can form a side dish to any of the rice dishes, Moin-moin, Ewa, Asaro, Dodo or Boli.

Roasted Meat

Serves 6-8

Ingredients:
- 12 pieces Meat/Chicken or 1.5Kg weight
- 1 Medium chopped onion
- 1 ½ Chicken 3 Maggi stock cubes
- 1 ½ tsp Mild curry powder
- 1 tsp All purpose seasoning
- 2 tsp Thyme
- ½ tsp Garlic powder
- 2 tsp Chilli powder
- 350mls Water
- ½ tsp Salt

Equipment:
- Medium saucepan
- Baking tray
- Stirring spoon
- Kitchen foil
- Slotted spoon
- Colander
- Oven

Cooking guide:

Step 1:
- Boil:
  - Rinse the meat/chicken in cold water and place in the saucepan
  - Add the onion, curry powder, all purpose seasoning, thyme, garlic powder, chilli powder
  - Crush in the chicken and Maggi stock cubes
  - Add 350mls of water
  - Allow all to marinate in the saucepan covered for 1 hour
  - Cover askew and cook at medium heat for 25 minutes (35 minutes if tough meat is bought) stirring frequently
- Preheat the oven to 170°C/350°F/gas 4

Step 2:
- Strain the meat once cooked into the colander with the slotted spoon, keeping aside the stock
- Line the baking tray with foil and grease with oil
- Place all the meat on the tray and drizzle some stock and oil over the top
- Roast in the oven for 30 minutes until golden, turning half-way

Serving Suggestions
Eat alone as a snack hot or cold. Alternatively it can be served with Gari, Fried and Jollof rice, Dodo, Boli, Ewa or Moin-moin.

Agbado

Serves 6-8

Ingredients:
- 4 large Agbado
- 1.5l Water
- ½ tsp Salt
- 30mls Vegetable/Sunflower oil

Equipment:
- Large saucepan/pressure cooker
- Oven
- Baking trays
- Kitchen foil

Cooking guide:

Step 1:
- Remove the husks off the corn
- Break each portion into half
- If roasting the corn then pre-heat the oven at 170°C/350°F/gas 4

Step 2:
- Rinse each corn on the cob and place in the pressure cooker
- Add the water and salt
- Cover and cook for 45 minutes if making boiled corn on the cob. However, if making roasted corn boil for 20 minutes only and remove
- If using a regular saucepan then boil the corn for about an hour. Only 30 minutes if roasting the corn.

Step 3:
- Line the baking tray with foil
- Grease the corn and tray with oil
- Roast all the corn on the cob together for 35 minutes

Step 4:
- Once prepared whether boiled or roasted, remove and serve

Serving Suggestions
Eat the Agbado hot and with butter, or just plain if you prefer.

Puff Puff

Serves 6-8

Ingredients:
- 500g Self-raising flour
- 400mls Fresh milk
- 85g Caster Sugar
- 1 tsp Vanilla essence
- 1 Large egg
- 1 Pinch salt
- 500mls Vegetable oil

Equipment:
- Large mixing bowl
- Wooden spoon
- Medium frying pan
- Colander
- Sieve

Cooking guide:

Step 1:
- Sieve and mix flour and sugar in bowl
- Gradually add milk mixing continuously with wooden spoon
- Add egg, salt and vanilla essence
- Mix thoroughly
- Leave to stand for at least 2 hours (preferably leave overnight in the fridge)

Step 2:
- Place medium pan with oil on medium heat
- Test heat with small drop of batter, it should rise if the oil is hot enough
- Deep fry by dropping spoonfuls of batter into the oil to make balls
- Fry until golden-brown on each side, turning as is appropriate
- Place in colander to cool
- Continue until the mixture is all fried, the oil may need topping up

Serving Suggestions

Eat alone hot or cold as a snack.

Chin Chin

Serves 6-8

Ingredients:
- 3 cups Plain flour
- ¾ cup Melted margarine
- 1 Large egg
- ¾ tsp Baking powder
- 40mls Water
- 40mls Fresh Milk
- 4 tbsp Caster sugar
- 500mls Vegetable oil

Equipment:
- Large mixing bowl
- Wooden spoon
- Slotted spoon
- Chopping board
- Rolling pin
- Medium frying pan
- Medium knife
- Sieve

Cooking guide:

Step 1:
- Sieve and mix flour, sugar and baking powder in bowl
- Add water, milk, margarine and egg and mix in
- Use hands to knead mixture

Step 2:
- Dust chopping board with flour
- Place dough on chopping board and roll out
- Make the dough roughly square or rectangular
- Start at one edge cutting 1cm thick strips
- With each strip cut 0.5cm pieces

Step 3:
- Heat oil on medium heat
- Test a piece to see if it floats
- Add as many pieces that will fit the pan
- Heat may need to be turned down and up intermittently to ensure that the chin chin does not burn
- Once evenly golden brown remove and lay out on a baking tray

Serving Suggestions
Allow to cool and consume as a tasty snack, with a cold drink.

Gari

Serves 1

Ingredients:
- 1/3 cup Gari
- 1 ¼ cups Water
- 1-2 tsp Sugar

Equipment:
- Bowl
- Spoon

Preparation guide:

Steps:
- Place the gari in a bowl
- Add the water and sugar
- Stir and enjoy

Serving Suggestions:
Enjoy this simple dish with Moin-moin, Akara or alone.
Options also include adding some evaporated milk to
the Gari. This has the tendency to swell and absorb
all the water so consume as soon as is made. You can
always add some more water if required.

Shuku-Shuku

Serves 4-6

Ingredients:
- 1 cup Desiccated coconut
- 3 medium Eggs
- ½ cup Self-raising flour
- ¼ cup Caster sugar

Equipment:
- Medium mixing bowl
- Mixing spoon
- 2 Baking trays
- Oven

Cooking Guide:

Step 1:
- Preheat the oven at 150°C/300°F/gas 3
- Grease 2 baking trays

Step 2:
- Crack the eggs into the bowl
- Add the caster sugar
- Add the coconut
- Mix in the flour using the wooden spoon

Step 3:
- Separate mixture into 12 equal pieces on the baking tray
- Place the tray in the oven on the middle and lower levels
- Bake for 20 minutes

Step 4:
- Leave to stand for 10 minutes

Serving Suggestions
Enjoy as a snack or as dessert.

Glossary

Akara => Savoury fried black-eyed beans cake

Amala => Yam flour cooked with boiling water, used to make the dishes we commonly call solid. Usually eaten with ones natural fork – the hand! Topped with the soup of your choice

Asaro => Mashed yam mixed with tomato-based sauce

Boli => Roasted yellow plantain

Crayfish => These are small freshwater decapods crustacean that resemble a lobster

Dindin => This is actually an adjective used to describe a fried dish

Dodo => Fried yellow plantain

Eba => Gari mixed with boiling water creates this staple known as solid, enjoyed most eaten by hand

Efo Riro => This is a spinach soup

Efo with Egusi => This is a spinach soup with the ground melon seed

Egusi => Melon seed, usually grounded

Elubo => Yam flour

Ewa => Cooked beans, which can be either black-eyed beans or Nigerian beans

Eyin Dindin => Spicy scrambled egg

Fried Rice => This is the yellow rice which is tasty but not spicy

Gari => Cassava grates

Gbegiri => This is a black-eyed beans soup

Igbako => Wooden curved serving dish used to serve dishes such as Amala and Iyan, again here it can easily be substituted for a side plate

Ila => This is the term for Okra when it is cooked

Isu => This is cooked yam and can be fried or boiled

Jollof Rice => This is the famous red rice that can be made as spicy as is desired

Moin-moin => Savoury boiled black-eyed beans cake

Obe ata => This is a stew usually made with an assortment of meat and chicken. The recipe can easily be adapted to create a fish or vegetarian version

Ogi => This is Pap, and can be bought either wet or dry

Ojojo => Grated and fried yam, a little like Nigerian hash browns

Orogun => Wooden stick, which if needed can be substituted for a wooden spoon which can be easily bought in most supermarkets

Afterword

Nigerian cuisine over the years, has evolved under the influence of inter-continental trade to incorporate ever more diverse flavours. Nigeria is home to a variety of cultures and people with each area possessing its own 'regional favourites' when it comes to food. This book gives a whistle-stop tour through some of the most well-known traditional dishes gracing the tables of Nigerians everyday.

At the heart of Nigerian cuisine are the exotic raw ingredients, herbs and spices which form the foundation of any exquisite Nigerian dish. They can readily be found in the inner city market places, ethnic food stores, and increasingly more and more in most of the well-known supermarket giant chains. Why not look out for them the next time you are out and about?

About the Author

Now a little bit about me. I have a mother who loves to cook and she does it so well. Every weekend when we would do the bulk of our cooking mum had one rule and one rule only! Whenever she was in the kitchen, we the kids had to be in the kitchen also. It was annoying then, but trust me I thank her now. It was from there my interest in cooking started. I remember watching intently, looking at exactly what she did and how she did it. I've adapted some of those best loved recipes, somewhat, over the years, which have culminated in the recipes you see in 'Quintessentially'.

I grew up as the second of four children to my parents and was born in Nigeria. We speak one of the 3 main native Nigerian languages known as Yoruba. We have since relocated to the United Kingdom more than twenty years ago and I did most of my pre-university education in Edinburgh, Scotland. I studied Medicine in a conjoint course between the universities of St Andrews, Scotland and Manchester, England. I currently work as a Doctor in the northwest of England. I love seeing my friends, watching movies, cooking dancing and going on holiday too when I get the chance.

Index

CPSIA information can be obtained
at www.ICGtesting.com
Printed in the USA
2762LVUK00005B

9 781467 880091